**DATE DUE**

PowerKids Readers:

# The Bilingual Library of the United States of America™

# WISCONSIN

**DEAN GALIANO**

TRADUCCIÓN AL ESPAÑOL: MARÍA CRISTINA BRUSCA

The Rosen Publishing Group's
PowerKids Press™ & **Editorial Buenas Letras**™
New York

Published in 2006 by The Rosen Publishing Group, Inc.
29 East 21st Street, New York, NY 10010

First Edition

Photo Credits: Cover © Joseph Fire/Index Stock Imagery, Inc.; p. 5 © Joe Sohm/The Image Works; p. 7 © 2002 Geoatlas; p. 9 © David Muench/Corbis; p. 11 courtesy National Museum of the American Indian, Smithsonian Institution, N26799, photo by Col. Frank C. Churchill; pp. 13, 31 (Settlers) © Science Museum/SSPL/The Image Works; p. 15 Library of Congress Prints and Photographs Division; pp. 17, 31 (Ingalls Wilder, Wright, O'Keefe) © Bettmann/Corbis; p. 19 © Ricard Price/Getty Images; p. 21 © Scott Witte/Index Stock Imagery, Inc.; p. 23 © Harry How/Getty Images; p. 25 © Nicolas Russell/Getty Images; pp. 26, 30 (Badger State) © Uwe Walz/Corbis; p. 30 (Capital) © Richard Cummins/Corbis; p. 30 (Wood Violet) © Buddy Mays/Corbis; p. 30 (Robin) © W. Perry Conway/Corbis; p. 30 (Sugar Maple) © Robert Estall/Corbis; p. 30 (Galena) © José Manuel Sanchis Calvete/Corbis; p. 31 (Welles) © John Springer Collection/Corbis; p. 31 (Rowlands) © Marcel Hartmann/Corbis; p. 31 (Heiden) © Duomo/Corbis; p. 31 (Hiking) © Don Mason/Corbis; p. 31 (Pulp) © Dan Lamont/Corbis

Library of Congress Cataloging-in-Publication Data

Galiano, Dean.
  Wisconsin / Dean Galiano ; traducción al español, María Cristina Brusca.—1st ed.
     p. cm. — (The bilingual library of the United States of America)
  Includes bibliographical references and index.
  ISBN 1-4042-3115-3 (library binding)
  1. Wisconsin—Juvenile literature. I. Title. II. Series.
  F581.3.G355 2006
  977.5-dc22
                                                    2005032649

Manufactured in the United States of America

Due to the changing nature of Internet links, Editorial Buenas Letras has developed an online list of Web sites related to the subject of this book. This site is updated regularly. Please use this link to access the list:

http://www.buenasletraslinks.com/ls/wisconsin

# Contents

# Contenido

## Welcome to Wisconsin

These are the flag and the seal of Wisconsin. The pictures on the state seal honor the trades that built Wisconsin. These are mining, farming, manufacturing, and ocean travel.

---

## Bienvenidos a Wisconsin

Estos son la bandera y el escudo de Wisconsin. El dibujo del escudo del estado honra los oficios que sustentaron a Wisconsin. Éstos son minería, agricultura y ganadería, manufactura y navegación.

Wisconsin Flag and State Seal

Bandera y escudo de Wisconsin

## Wisconsin Geography

Wisconsin is in the north-central United States. Wisconsin borders the states of Minnesota, Iowa, Illinois, and Michigan.

---

## Geografía de Wisconsin

Wisconsin está en la zona central del norte del país. Wisconsin linda con los estados de Minnesota, Iowa, Illinois y Michigan.

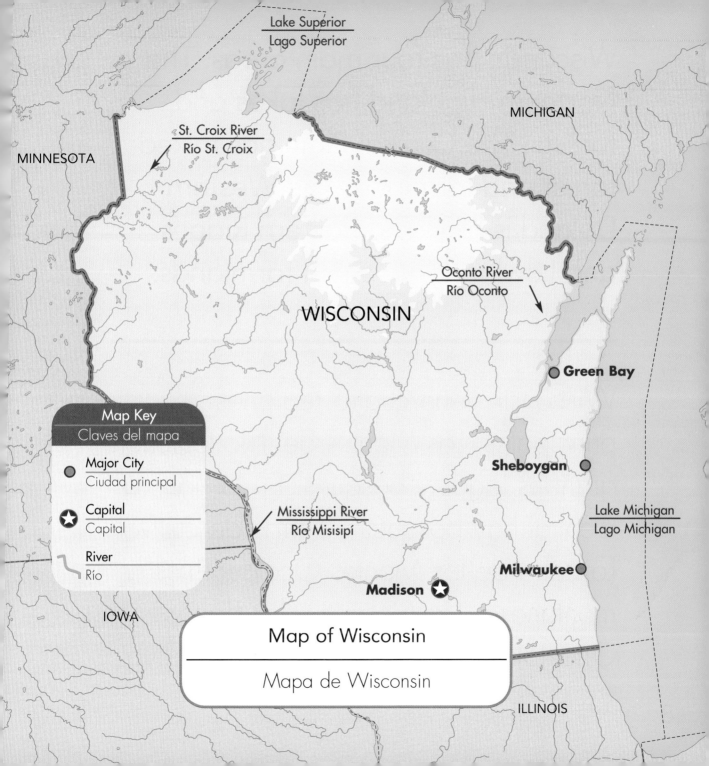

Lake Superior
Lago Superior

MICHIGAN

MINNESOTA

St. Croix River
Río St. Croix

WISCONSIN

Oconto River
Río Oconto

● Green Bay

Sheboygan ●

Lake Michigan
Lago Michigan

**Map Key**
Claves del mapa

● Major City
Ciudad principal

⭐ Capital
Capital

〰 River
Río

Mississippi River
Río Misisipí

Milwaukee ●

Madison ⭐

IOWA

**Map of Wisconsin**

Mapa de Wisconsin

ILLINOIS

Wisconsin has four main areas. The Northern Highland has lakes and forests. The Central Plain has mixed forest and farmland. The Western Upland is hilly. The Eastern Ridges and Lowlands have rich farmlands.

---

Wisconsin tiene cuatro regiones principales. Los Montes del Norte tienen grandes lagos y bosques. En la Llanura Central hay bosques y tierras de cultivo. La zona de los Montes Occidentales es montañosa. Las Colinas y los Llanos Orientales tienen ricas tierras de cultivo.

Wisconsin Dells in Southern Wisconsin

Barrancos en el sur de Wisconsin

## Wisconsin History

In 1634, French explorer Jean Nicolet became the first European to visit Wisconsin. The area was home to many Native American nations such as the Ojibwa, Dakota, and Potawatomi.

---

## Historia de Wisconsin

En 1637, el explorador francés Jean Nicolet fue el primer europeo en llegar a Wisconsin. La región era el hogar de muchas naciones nativoamericanas como las Ojibwa, Dakota y Potawatomi.

An Old Potawatomi Woman
___

Una anciana de la tribu Potawatomi

Wisconsin came under the control of the United States after the American Revolution. Rich minerals were discovered in the 1810s. Many settlers moved to the area to work in mining jobs.

---

Después de la Revolución Americana, Wisconsin pasó al dominio de los Estados Unidos. En la década de 1810, se descubrieron ricos yacimientos de minerales. Muchos colonos llegaron a la región para trabajar en las minas.

Mining on Lake Superior in 1855

Minería en el lago Superior, en 1855

In 1832, Native American chief Black Hawk, of the Sauk tribe, fought a war with U.S. troops in Wisconsin. He had been forced off his land by the U.S. government. Black Hawk wanted to get back the land for his people.

---

En 1832, el jefe Halcón Negro (*Black Hawk*), de la tribu Sauk, condujo en Wisconsin una guerra contra las tropas de los Estados Unidos. Su pueblo había sido expulsado de sus tierras por el gobierno de E.U.A. Halcón Negro quería recuperar su tierra.

## Chief Black Hawk

El cacique Halcón Negro

Robert Marion La Follette, Jr. was governor of Wisconsin from 1901–1906 and senator from 1906–1925. La Follette helped control business so that working people would be treated fairly.

---

Robert Marion La Follette Jr. fue gobernador de Wisconsin de 1901 a 1906 y senador de 1906 a 1925. La Follette ayudó a regular las industrias para que los trabajadores fueran tratados con justicia.

Robert Marion La Follete

## Living in Wisconsin

Many people in Wisconsin work in dairy farms. Dairy goods such as milk and cheese are important to Wisconsin. Wisconsin produces more cheese than does any other state.

---

## La vida en Wisconsin

Muchos wisconsinitas trabajan en granjas lecheras. Los productos lácteos como la leche y el queso son importantes para Wisconsin. Wisconsin produce más queso que cualquier otro estado del país.

Dairy Farm in Thorp, Wisconsin

Granja lechera en Thorp, Wisconsin

Papermaking is an important Wisconsin business. The forests of northern Wisconsin provide the wood pulp needed to make paper. Wisconsin is the leading papermaking state in the United States.

---

La industria papelera es un negocio importante en Wisconsin. Los bosques del norte del estado proporcionan la pulpa de madera que se necesita para hacer papel. Wisconsin es líder en la fabricación de papel en los Estados Unidos.

Paper Factory in Wisconsin

Fábrica de papel en Wisconsin

Football is a well-liked sport in Wisconsin. The Packers are located in Green Bay. The Packers are a cause for pride to many people in Wisconsin. They have won the Super Bowl three times.

---

El fútbol americano es un deporte muy apreciado en Wisconsin. Green Bay es el hogar de los Packers. Muchos wisconsinitas se sienten orgullosos de los Packers. Este equipo ha ganado el Super Bowl tres veces.

The Green Bay Packers Football Team

Equipo de fútbol americano Green Bay Packers

Many people visit Wisconsin lakes during the summer. The scenic beauty of northern Wisconsin makes the area a popular place for outdoor sports such as swimming, hiking, and hunting.

---

Mucha gente visita los lagos de Wisconsin durante el verano. La belleza del paisaje del norte de Wisconsin atrae a muchos amantes de los deportes al aire libre como la natación, la caza y la pesca.

Fishing on Lake Tenderfoot, Wisconsin

Pesca en el lago Tenderfoot, Wisconsin

# Activity:
## Let's Draw a Badger
The Badger is Wisconsin's State Animal

# Actividad:
## Dibujemos un tejón

El tejón es el animal del estado de Wisconsin

**1**

Look at the picture of the badger before you start. First draw a triangle and then draw a half oval.

Antes de comenzar, mira la foto del tejón. Comienza por dibujar un triángulo y luego dibuja la mitad de un óvalo.

**2**

Add a second triangle for the badger's head. The bottom of this triangle should point down and to the left.

Agrega un segundo triángulo en el lugar de la cabeza del tejón. El triángulo tiene que apuntar hacia abajo y hacia la izquierda.

**3**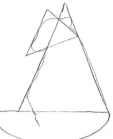

Use the guide shapes as a starting point to draw the head and the body of the badger.

Dibuja la cabeza y el cuerpo del tejón siguiendo las formas de guía.

**4**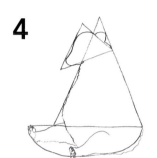

Now add the two back legs of the badger.

Ahora, agrega las dos patas traseras del tejón.

**5**

Add the badger's eye and the outline of the badger's arms.

Agrega el ojo y los brazos del tejón.

**6**

Now shade the badger as shown.

Sombrea el dibujo del tejón siguiendo el modelo.

# Timeline

# Cronología

| | Timeline | | Cronología |
|---|---|---|---|
| **1634** | Frenchman Jean Nicolet is the first known European to reach Wisconsin. | | El francés, Jean Nicolet es el primer europeo en alcanzar Wisconsin. |
| **1673** | Louis Jolliet and Jacques Marquette discover the Mississippi River. | | Louis Jolliet y Jacques Marquette descubren el río Misisipí. |
| **1763** | Wisconsin becomes part of British colonial territory. | | Wisconsin pasa a formar parte del territorio colonial británico. |
| **1783** | The United States takes ownership of the Wisconsin area. | | Los Estados Unidos toman posesión de la región de Wisconsin. |
| **1832** | Black Hawk War. | | Guerra de Halcón Negro. |
| **1835** | The first steamboat arrives at Milwaukee. | | Llega a Milwaukee el primer barco de vapor. |
| **1848** | Wisconsin becomes the nation's thirtieth state. | | Wisconsin se convierte en el trigésimo estado. |
| **1861–1865** | More than 90,000 men from Wisconsin fight for the Union in the Civil War. | | Más de 90,000 hombres, oriundos de Wisconsin, se unen al ejército de la Unión para luchar en la Guerra Civil. |
| **1917** | The capitol building is finished in Madison, Wisconsin. | | Se termina la construcción del capitolio en Madison, Wisconsin. |

# Wisconsin Events

### January
Martin Luther King, Jr. Celebration in Milwaukee

### March
Irish Fest in New London

### May
Cinco de Mayo Springfest in West Allis

### June
RiverSplash in Milwaukee
Polish Fest in Milwaukee

### July
German Fest in Milwaukee

### August
Wisconsin State Fair in West Allis

### September
Oktoberfest in La Crosse
Indian Summer Festival in Milwaukee

### October
Scandinavian Festival in Superior

### November
Hmong New Year celebration in Schofield

# Eventos en Wisconsin

### Enero
Celebraciones Martín Luther King Jr., en Milwaukee

### Marzo
Fiesta irlandesa, en New London

### Mayo
Fiesta del Cinco de Mayo, en West Allis

### Junio
RiverSplash, en Milwaukee
Fiesta polaca, en Milwaukee

### Julio
Fiesta alemana, en Milwaukee

### Agosto
Feria del estado de Wisconsin, en West Allis

### Septiembre
Oktoberfest, en La Crosse
Festival del verano indio, en Milwaukee

### Octubre
Festival escandinavo, en Superior

### Noviembre
Celebración del año nuevo Hmong, en Schofield.

# Wisconsin Facts/Datos sobre Wisconsin

<u>Population</u>
5.3 million

<u>Población</u>
5.3 millones

<u>Capital</u>
Madison

<u>Capital</u>
Madison

<u>State Motto</u>
"Forward"

<u>Lema del estado</u>
Adelante

<u>State Flower</u>
Wood violet

<u>Flor del estado</u>
Violeta

<u>State Bird</u>
Robin

<u>Ave del estado</u>
Petirrojo

<u>State Nickname</u>
The Badger State

<u>Mote del estado</u>
Estado del Tejón

<u>State Tree</u>
Sugar maple

<u>Árbol del estado</u>
Arce azucarero

<u>State Song</u>
"On Wisconsin"

<u>Canción del estado</u>
"Adelante Wisconsin"

<u>State Mineral</u>
Galena

<u>Piedra preciosa</u>
Galena

# Famous Wisconsinites/Wisconsinitas famosos

**Laura Ingalls Wilder**
*(1867–1957)*

Writer

Escritora

**Frank Lloyd Wright**
*(1867–1959)*

Architect

Arquitecto

**Georgia O'Keeffe**
*(1887–1986)*

Painter

Pintora

**Orson Welles**
*(1915–1985)*

Actor

Actor

**Gena Rowlands**
*(1930–   )*

Actress

Actriz

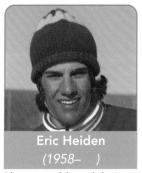

**Eric Heiden**
*(1958–   )*

Olympic gold medal winner

Campeón olímpico

## Words to Know/Palabras que debes saber

border

frontera

hiking

caminata

pulp

pulpa

settlers

colonos

31

# Here are more books to read about Wisconsin:
## Otros libros que puedes leer sobre Wisconsin:

**In English/En inglés:**
*B Is for Badger: A Wisconsin Alphabet*
*Discover America State By State.*
by Kathy-Jo Wargin, Renee Graef
Sleeping Bear Press, 2004

*Wisconsin: The Badger State*
*World Almanac Library of the States*
by Rachel Barenblat, Jean Craven
Gareth Stevens Publishing, 2001

Words in English: 324

Palabras en español: 366

# Index

# Índice